THE DAWN OF
UNIVERSAL HISTORY

The Dawn of Universal History

RAYMOND ARON

Translated from the French by
DOROTHY PICKLES

FREDERICK A. PRAEGER, *Publishers*
NEW YORK

Published in the United States of America in 1961
by Praeger Paperbacks, Inc.,
64 University Place, New York 3, N.Y.

English Translation
© 1961 by George Weidenfeld and Nicolson Ltd

Library of Congress catalog card number 61-7815

PRINTED IN GREAT BRITAIN

The Dawn of Universal History

*Based on the fourth Herbert Samuel Lecture
delivered on 18th February, 1960,
under the auspices of the
British Friends of the
Hebrew University of Jerusalem.*

A FEW WORDS of explanation are called for, I think, concerning the title of this essay and the unfortunate impression that it has undoubtedly created in the mind of the reader. My choice of subject—a subject that I shall deal with only sketchily—is attributable to my English publisher. A year or two ago, this publisher, who has brought out a series of books dealing with different epochs of our civilization, asked me to write a history of the world from 1914. I replied immediately that no reputable historian would undertake such a task. We have lived through only part of the history of these years. We have followed it from different places and under the influence of our different passions and prejudices. None of us has a complete picture or has mastered the immense mass of scattered material, or has been able as yet to achieve a rational understanding of events so crammed with human suffering, unprecedented crimes and immeasurable promise.

On reflection, I qualified my objection that no reputable historian would have the temerity to accede to such request by pointing out that I was not a historian. And I asked myself whether as a philosopher, perhaps, or a sociologist, I could not write a brief study of the history of our time bringing out its originality and emphasizing what I have called the dawn of universal history. For never before in history have the so-called higher civilizations lived through the same history. For the first time, we can legitimately speak of 'human society'.

I shall include in this essay a few of the ideas which will form the introduction and the conclusion to the book that I agreed to write. I am fully aware that this study will probably meet with severe criticism from many of the philosophers and historians among my university colleagues. In the more traditional English universities, sociology is not yet a fully accepted subject, or else it is called by some less Americanized name, such as anthropology. As for the philosophy of history, whether deriving from Bossuet, Hegel, Marx or Toynbee, it is still, for the most part, held to be less of a scientific than a literary exercise, an exercise to which writers, but not thinkers, may devote their attention. Let me say in advance and in my own defence, first, that nobody is more conscious than I of how uncertain and vulnerable what I have to say will be. My work will not be a narrative like that of Thucydides (the events that I have to deal with are too numerous and too incoherent). Nor will it be a synthesis like Burckardt's work on the Italian Renaissance. It will be an essay and will claim to be no more. Its perspectives will be restricted by the inevitable personal limitations of the author and it will be coloured by the experiences and hopes of a man formed by a particular country, a particular generation and a particular intellectual system.

Can I really be reproached for writing so unambitious an essay, when, consciously or unconsciously, we are all helping to write it? The scholar can perhaps look at past ages from the viewpoint of a pure spectator. The historian of Athens or Sparta, of Rome or Carthage, of the Pope, the Emperor, the Holy Roman Empire and the French monarchy may not feel personally involved in the passions that move the actors on his stage. He may succeed in reaching an equally detached understanding of all combatants, of their common beliefs and conflicting interests, of the achievements and disasters of which they were the unwitting architects. But when we open our newspaper, or vote for a candidate in an election, we deliberately involve ourselves in a particular period of time. Anyone who attempts to see clearly what an Englishman or a Frenchman of the twentieth century has lived through or undergone must also be interpreting 'the world from 1914'. The interpretation of the twentieth century which I am about to offer, will, I hope, be less fragmentary, less emotionally subjective. I shall deal first with the method that I propose to adopt.

PART I

FROM THE BEGINNING of the nineteenth century, every European generation has believed in the uniqueness of its own period. Does the very persistence of this conviction in itself indicate that it was unfounded? Or was it rather a kind of premonition, the truth of which has been borne out by our own generation, and which must, therefore, have been false in the case of our predecessors? If we hesitate to ascribe error to so many generations, or rather to every generation but our own, can we suggest a third hypothesis, namely, that all of them have been right, not individually, but regarded as a whole, and not always in the ways that they thought?

In other words, it would seem to be a fact, or at least a plausible hypothesis, that the last century has seen a kind of revolution, or more precisely a *mutation*, which began before the nineteenth century, but whose rate of change has accelerated during the past few decades.

From the beginning of the last century onwards, every generation and every thinker has tried to define this historical mutation. Saint-Simon and Auguste Comte wrote of 'the industrial society',

Alexis de Tocqueville of democratic society and Karl Marx of capitalist society. If we go back to the great theorists of the first half of the last century—from whom we derive our ideologies, if not our ideas—and compare their diagnoses and their prophecies with what has actually happened between their time and our own, we shall be able to reach a tentative definition of what I have called a historical mutation.

Let us begin with the school of Saint-Simon and Auguste Comte, who are now once again becoming fashionable, for the very comprehensible reason that the building up of large-scale industry on both sides of the iron curtain has at last compelled observers to recognize the existence of a certain type of society, of which the Soviet and Western systems represent two different species or variants. Why not describe this form of society as industrial, since its characteristic is the development of industry?

This was, indeed, the central hypothesis of Saint-Simon and Auguste Comte. Both watched a new society in process of construction before their eyes, a society to which Europe had given birth, and which they described as industrial. The essential characteristics of this new society were more accurately described by Auguste Comte than by either Saint-Simon or even the Saint-Simonians. And although few today read the works of the founder of positivism, and still fewer devote any serious study to them, it is his definition of industrial society which we shall take as our starting point.

Like Saint-Simon, Comte stresses the contrast between producers—industrialists, farmers and bankers—and the political and military *élites* who, in a society devoted to peaceful activities, represent survivals from a feudal and theological past. Industrial society, as indeed all human society, has henceforth as its first objective the exploitation of natural resources. Wars, conquest and Caesars belong to the past. In the view of the philosophers of history, Napoleon, for all his genius, was guilty of the most serious of all crimes—that of being an anachronism. Roman conquests had a meaning. They were creative, because they prepared the way for a unified world in which the Christian religion was to spread, and because communities dedicated to war would at some point achieve peace through the victory of the strongest. In our time, however, conquest cannot be justified, because it no longer serves any purpose, because the spontaneous resistance and ultimate triumph of the people has revealed the error of Napoleon. When he came to power, the peoples of Europe were grateful for all that the French Revolution had done for them, but he transformed that heritage of sympathy into hatred.

Arguing with a dogmatism that some will feel to be characteristic of sociologists, Auguste Comte deduces the consequences, all the consequences, that follow from this change of objective. Henceforth it is labour, not war, which constitutes the supreme good. It is through men's labour that a society's *cadres* and leaders are formed, that individual prestige is generally recognized and individual status assured. There must, therefore, be freedom of labour. There must be no more rigid classification of families on the basis of class or occupation. Mobility must be the rule from one generation to another. Henceforth individuals are entitled to hope that their place in society will be determined on the basis of merit, without reference to the position of their parents. To Comte, the wage-earning class represented, not a modern form of slavery or serfdom, but the promise of individual liberation and of social mobility. Europe, or, more precisely, the nations of Western Europe—England, France, Italy, Spain and Germany—constitute the vanguard. The European nations were in advance of others in the pursuit of what was henceforth to be the common objective, namely, the exploitation of the resources of this planet, the creation of an industrial society and the unification within one single peaceful community of peoples dispersed throughout five continents. According to the high priest of positivism, Europe's advance did not confer privileges so much as impose obligations, and Auguste Comte warned his contemporaries against succumbing to the temptation of colonial adventures. Again and again he denounced the conquest of Algeria and even expressed the hope that the Arabs would 'pursue the French with vigour', if the French lacked the intelligence or the moral sense to withdraw of their own accord.

It is easy enough to ridicule Auguste Comte's prophecies and many have done so. He made a great mistake when he proclaimed that the days of colonial wars and colonial conquest were ended. But if he is regarded, not as a prophet, but as a counsellor of princes and peoples, then his words were certainly wiser than the trend of events. He did not predict the future accurately. He predicted what it would have been if history had been made by the good and the wise.

He used to say that the industrial society in process of spreading throughout Western Europe is, and must be, an example to the human race. He was right at least on this point. But he was certainly wrong in regarding Europe as the centre of the universe, in failing to recognize the specific characteristics of other civilizations, in believing that the forms of political organization and religious belief were rigorously determined by the type of social organization, and so in overlooking the essential permanence of what he called theological or metaphysical modes of thought. In his perception of the relation between work and war, of the relation between the exploitation of natural resources and the exploitation of man, and of the nature of the revolution that governments and people have come painfully and at long last to accept, he was undeniably clear-sighted and accurate. Wars between industrial societies are both ruinous and sterile. Non-industrial, or, as we call them, under-developed societies, are obliged to model themselves on industrial societies and so, in a sense, Europe does, as he said, serve as an example. But Europe would be wrong, in the Comtian view, if she were to force them to follow her example by using her temporary advance to reopen the era of great conquests. What purpose is served by killing, enslaving, pillaging? Gold and silver no longer constitute real wealth. Wealth consists of rationally organized labour. In the distant past, slavery was necessary in order to impose the habit of regular effort on men naturally prone to idleness or to lack of concentration. But Europeans are now so habituated to the concept of the rationalization of labour that compulsion is no longer necessary. Wars, like colonial conquest, are, therefore, anachronisms. If we agree with Auguste Comte that men do not make war for its own sake or simply owing to their passion for conquest, then we must regard wars today as irrational, even though they have continued to exist. If the major objective of industrial societies is to achieve well-being through work, as spokesmen of both Soviet and Western society allege today, then the two European wars which have occurred during the course of this century were useless and there ought not to be a third.

Let us now consider another great theorist, who belongs to the generation following that of Auguste Comte. Karl Marx also recognized the existence of a historical mutation and, although he used a different vocabulary and different concepts, he emphasized the same essential fact, namely, that the forces of production had developed more rapidly than in any preceding century and this he saw as the achievement of bourgeois capitalism.

Within the space of a few decades, the triumphant bourgeoisie had brought about changes in the conditions and the methods of collective labour greater than any made by the leaders of feudal or military society during the previous thousand years.

There is agreement between the high priests of socialism and of positivism regarding the fundamental difference between modern and traditional societies. Both men consider that the uniqueness of modern society lies in the pride of place accorded to work, to the application of science to the techniques of production, and in the resultant increase in collective resources. The major difference between their two theories is that Marx attaches fundamental importance to the conflict between employers and employed, whilst Auguste Comte considers this to be a phenomenon of secondary importance, a symptom of social disintegration that will be corrected as organization improves.

Marx tends to explain everything—poverty in the midst of plenty in spite of the increased powers of production, the alienation of the workers, the despotism of the property-owning minority—as being due to the conflict between employers and employed, the class struggle between capitalists and the proletariat. His vision of the future of capitalism is, therefore, apocalyptic. The conflict between capitalists and proletariat will be intensified to the point at which an explosion ultimately occurs. Marx then sketches in outline an idyllic picture of the post-capitalist regime. He nowhere describes it, but he points out, by way of contrast, the benefits that it will confer. The specific characteristics of capitalism, namely, private ownership of the means of production, the capitalist minority's possession of economic power and, through intermediaries, of political power, are responsible for social inequalities, the exploitation of man by man and working-class alienation. It follows that, with the elimination of private property, and with the proletarian revolution, the prehistory of humanity will come to an end and a new era will be opened up, in which social progress will no longer depend on violence and political revolutions.

On the essential point of difference between Karl Marx and Auguste Comte, the former seems to me to have been right in the short term, but wrong in the long term. Conflicts between employers and employed, either within the industry or about the distribution of the national income, have not been decisive and they were, on the whole, more serious during the initial phases of industrialization than they have been in mature industrial societies. The working classes, organized in trade unions and protected by social legislation, often represented in Parliament by powerful Socialist parties, continue to press their claims, but they have been converted to peaceful and legal methods. They do not want a revolution which would establish the dictatorship of the proletariat. They are not really clear as to what a proletarian revolution would be. In their view, as in that of most observers, there is clear proof that private ownership of the means of production, as it exists today in Western society, does not prevent either the development of productive forces or a continued rise in the standard of living of the masses. Whatever conclusions can be reached regarding the relative efficiency of the Soviet and Western regimes, it is evident that the one does not mean plenty for the masses nor the other poverty. Indeed, the differences between the two systems are less striking inside the factory than outside, in the sphere of the organization of the State and of the administration. There is in our industrial society, as Comte claimed, a technical and bureaucratic hierarchy in which there is a place for free workers.

In the twentieth century, the predominant conflicts have been national and imperial and it is these that have determined the course of history. Auguste Comte and Karl Marx did not misunderstand the nature of the historical mutation that was taking place before their eyes, but it is arguable that they underestimated the extent to which the traditional historical phenomena would persist—the rise and fall of empires, the rivalry of different systems, the beneficent or dangerous activities of great men.

In different ways, both underestimated the importance of the political factor. Marx wrote as if the power of the bourgeoisie constituted an adequate definition of the political aspect of capitalism and as if a socialist political system was adequately defined by the semi-mythological concept of the dictatorship of the proletariat. Auguste Comte was content to leave power in the hands of the managers responsible for production, trusting to the resistance of public opinion, that of women and of the proletariat, to prevent abuse of their control over working conditions. Both left out of account the possibility of an evolution along the lines suggested by Alexis de Tocqueville, who foresaw the development of a commercial and industrial society with increased social mobility and greater equality. This is, fundamentally, the direction in which modern societies are moving, though they are still free to choose between a

system in which a single individual rules despotic-
ally over millions whose individuality is sub-
merged in servitude and uniformity, and one based
on freedom for all, a freedom which may offer no
more material satisfaction and some degree of
mediocrity, but which protects the rights of
individual initiative, individual decision, and personal belief.

Sociological theorists have failed to take into
account the partial autonomy of the political order
and have argued as if history, by which they
meant the succession of wars and empires, victories
and defeats, was henceforth ended. But the present
century seems to me in 1960 to present two distinct
faces. On the one hand it has witnessed an intellectual, technical and economic revolution, which,
like some cosmic force, is carrying humanity
towards an unknown future; on the other it is in
many respects very like its predecessors. It is not
the first century to have seen great wars. On the
one hand, there is the need for progress; on the
other there is *history as usual*,[1] with its drama of
empires, armies and heroes.

The forces of change are clearly revealed in
statistics of intellectual and industrial production.
At the beginning of the century, the consumption

---

[1] In English in the original.

of petrol amounted to a few tons a year. Today, it amounts to a billion tons a year—I repeat, a billion tons—and it is increasing at the rate of 10 per cent every year. Fifty years ago, a great power would produce a few thousand tons of steel a year. Today the same amount represents no more than the annual increase in production. Robert Oppenheimer has quoted some figures that seem to me particularly striking in this context. He states that 90 per cent of all the scientific research workers who have existed since the beginning of time are still alive. This shows the acceleration of history, the rapidly increasing growth of the knowledge which is power, to return to the language of Auguste Comte.

Let us turn now to traditional history. At every turn the mind is baffled. Things happen and, once done, nothing can be undone. But how near some events have come to not happening! If the Germans had not sent two army corps to the East on the eve of the battle of the Marne, would there ever have been a miracle of the Marne? If the world crisis had not lasted for years, or if the English and French had used military means to prevent the German reoccupation of the Rhineland, would the last world war ever have happened? Without Churchill, would England ever have stood alone against the Third Reich? If Hitler had not attacked Russia in 1941, what would have been the subsequent course of the greatest of all the great wars? Traditional history is action; in other words it is made up of decisions taken by specific persons at specific times and in specific places. If a different man had been called on to take the decisions in the same circumstances, or if the same man had had to take them in different circumstances, the results might have been quite different. Yet nobody can determine either before or after the event the extent to which certain of these decisions, taken at particular times and in particular places, have affected the course of events.

Traditional history seems to be governed by chance and there is cruelty in it as well as grandeur. The blood of the innocents flows everywhere and the victories of princes are paid for by the sacrifices of the people. A world in which knowledge is power, on the other hand, is governed by the laws of necessity and the triumphs of the masses make those of individuals or of small groups look insignificant. I am tempted to imagine what the history of the thirty years' war—the thirty years from 1914 to 1945—would look like, if it had been written by Thucydides. Its first episode was compared by Toynbee and Thibaudet to the Peloponnesian War. (But did they realize, in 1918, that the peace of Versailles would turn out to be the truce of Nicias?) It would probably be necessary to fill in the gaps in the dramatic narrative by asking a Marx or a Colin Clark to write, not a narrative, but an analysis of the irresistible process of industrialization on our planet. In one sense, this process is no less dramatic than the story of the building up and the destruction of the Third Reich. Like a torrent it carries everything along with it, uprooting age-old customs, causing the growth of factories and tentacular towns, covering the entire planet with roads and railways, offering the masses the prospect of that plenty that privileged nations have shown to be attainable. But it begins by tearing men away from the protection afforded by beliefs and habits that have been handed down for centuries, and by subjecting millions of men, bereft of faith and law, to the uncertainties of an incomprehensible system governed by mysterious machines.

I do not know whether, in my book which is not yet written, I shall be able to convey to the reader these two facets, human action and necessity, what I have called 'drama' and what I have called 'the process,' *history as usual* and the special features brought into history by industrial society. But now that I have emphasized the differences between these two approaches to the history of our century, may I go on to try to indicate the numerous ways, fortuitous or inevitable, in which drama and the process have been combined to form the web of history as it has actually been woven? Let us try to look at the laws of industrial necessity in action as they have affected the drama of wars and empires. Let us see too how the industrial process has been affected by the actions of a few individuals who have influenced its form and shaped its features. After standing the dialectic doubly on its head, we can go on to ask whether the process will be able to continue without the drama.

PART II

AS I SEE IT, there are three ways, none of them exclusive, of arranging in logical sequence the succession of events and accidents, that is, of discovering the law of industrial evolution in the drama of great wars. The historian can use the state of the industrial system to explain either the origin of wars, or their course, or their results. I do not hold with the first method but I shall make considerable use here of the second and third.

The first method, that of Lenin and the Marxists, sees in the drama merely a spectacular episode in the process. The 1914 war is, on this theory, not an expression of the traditional nature of human history, but the inevitable consequence of capitalist contradictions and of rivalry between capitalist states. This is not the place to discuss in detail a theory that I have often discussed.[1] But it will perhaps help to make this essay more complete if I may be allowed to summarize this classical thesis—which still has more supporters than it deserves—by the three following propositions.

[1] c.f. for example, *War and Industrial Society*, Oxford University Press, London, 1958.

C

(1) Colonial imperialism, it is claimed, is merely the extreme form of capitalist expansion in that part of the world now called under-developed, in the continents with a traditional economy whose weakness has made them defenceless victims of the greed of large-scale concerns, of domination by European states.

(2) In this view, the peaceful division of the world into spheres of influence or colonial empires was impossible. Capitalists and capitalist systems were driven by their feverish search for profits, for markets for their products, for human labour to exploit and raw materials to develop. Capitalist economies were no more able to reach durable agreements for the sharing out of the planet than individualist capitalists within one country were able to agree on the sharing out of markets or the cessation of competition.

(3) Although the great war was waged on the old continent, and was apparently on this thesis, a specifically European conflict, its real cause, what was really at stake, was the

sharing-out of the planet. Unknowingly, Frenchmen, Germans and Englishmen died to increase the share of their respective countries in the other parts of the world.

In my view, the facts do not bear out these three propositions and in some respects they disprove them. Or at least, an impartial examination of the facts renders them suspect. Economic expansion in its different forms (the search for super-profits from the development of rich sources of raw materials; or from the exploitation of human labour; the search for markets for manufactured products, the attempt to keep privileges and keep out competitors), even if we suppose it to be essentially bound up with the capitalist system, does not automatically entail colonial conquest and the establishment of political sovereignty. The latter is useful or indispensable, in the economic sphere, only to keep out competitors and obtain advantages not admissible in conditions of free competition. The African territories, which the Western European countries were able to conquer with ease at the end of the nineteenth and the beginning of the twentieth centuries, account for only an infinitesimal fraction of the foreign trade of capitalist states and absorb only a small proportion of the capital which the old continent, as world banker, invested abroad. In these circumstances, how can we accept the proposition that colonial conquest is the extreme form, the inevitable expression, of an expansion which is inherent in capitalist economies?

The second proposition also seems to me arbitrary. It is well known that in internal markets competitors can often share out markets and thus suspend the working of the so-called inexorable law of competition. A division of the world into spheres of influence, an amicable settlement by the European nations of their quarrels over Africa would *a fortiori* have been easily achieved if what had been at stake had been mere commercial interest! But the European countries are each other's best customers precisely because they are industrially developed. The great capitalist companies regarded West or Equatorial Africa, Algeria or Morocco, as only marginal areas of their activity. German banks were less interested in Morocco than the Wilhelmstrasse would have liked them to be. It was the foreign offices which made co-operation between French and German capitalists impossible in Morocco. Diplomats thought in terms of power, not because they were concerned about commercial interests, or because spokesmen of commercial interests brought pressure to bear on them, but because they had read their history books and because for centuries that had been the rule of politics.

Finally, I am still waiting for someone to convince me that a war started by German and Slav rivalry in the Balkans, fought mainly in Europe and seen by the participants, from the day it broke out, as being solely concerned with power relationships within the European diplomatic system, had, in reality, different causes and different aims. It would need a great deal of ingenuity to prove that Africa and Asia were the cause of a war which began with the revolver shots that killed the Archduke of Austria. Why should the political status of Central and Eastern Europe be regarded as a less genuine reason for fighting than concern for distant lands?

To anyone who looks at the past without preconceived opinions, all the facts, indeed, point in one direction and justify a single conclusion, namely, that the causes of the 1914–1918 war conformed to historical tradition no less than preceding European wars and no less than the great war whose history was written by Thucydides and in which all the cities involved formed the Hellenic system, just as the states of the old continent made up the European international system. A balance of powers which breaks up into two coalitions, or in which one power threatens to establish its hegemony over the whole of the area, creates a situation which is, in itself, liable to lead to a ruthless war. At the end of the fifth century BC, Athens was endangering the liberties of the Greek cities. At the beginning of the twentieth century, Germany was similarly endangering the liberty of European nations. War to the death was not on that account inevitable, but, if war broke out, it was inevitable that other great powers should immediately feel that they were fighting for their freedom and for their existence.

The situation in the Balkans, which was the immediate cause of the explosion, was neither a pretext nor an opportunity to be seized. Austria-Hungary and Turkey were multi-national empires, the one a survival from a time when provinces belonged to sovereigns, the other built solely on conquest and maintained only by the power of the sword. But the balance of power was disturbed by the ultimate disintegration of these empires, and particularly by that of Austria-Hungary. Germany lost her principal ally, and millions of Slavs appeared likely to go over to the opposite camp. It is comprehensible that the Reich should have supported the dual empire in an adventure whose purpose was to ensure its safety, or at least to gain a respite, but which, in fact, ended in its death. It is equally comprehensible that, from the beginning of August 1914, Great Britain, and even more France, should have feared a German victory which would have entailed the loss of France's status as a great power and possibly the loss of French independence.

The 1914 war broke out in the industrial century but its beginnings were those of an ordinary war. It is the course of the war and its consequences which belong specifically to, and are characteristic of, the century in which it occurred.

The great war whose history was related by Thucydides was fought from beginning to end with the same weapons and, throughout its countless battles, apart from a few ingenious tricks during the Sicilian expedition, it was the heroism of the Greeks that stood out rather than their technical or tactical ingenuity. The thirty years' war of the twentieth century began with the revolver shot of Sarajevo, or with the 'bombardment of Belgrade by Austrian guns and ended with the atomic thunderclaps of Hiroshima and Nagasaki'. Between 1914 and 1945, the techniques of production and destruction had gone through several stages of evolution.

The first battles were fought with machine-guns, light horse-drawn cannon, and heavy artillery. The continuous front, the trenches, the accumulation of artillery, and the preparations which required ever-increasing numbers of cannon and ever-increasing amounts of munitions, are characteristic of the second phase, that of the bloody and sterile battles in which tens of thousands of men fell in order to hold a few miles of land whose possession or loss meant nothing. The last phase was characterized by motorized warfare, with thousands of aircraft, tanks and lorries, with the co-operation of air and armoured forces to which Hitler's *Wehrmacht* owed its spectacular triumphs of 1939 to 1941. The age of petrol had succeeded that of coal (though it had not replaced coal) and light metals were being used along with steel. But the qualitative superiority that one industrial country achieved over another was bound to be precarious. The battle for quantity—the race for men, arms, munitions — which had been the dominating characteristic of the first phase of this thirty years' war, was intensified during the second phase. With four thousand tanks and almost as many planes, Germany had put first Poland and then

France out of action and won some spectacular victories during the summer of 1941. But by 1944–45 the industrial machine of the anti-German coalition was working at full pressure and the Soviet and Anglo-American armies were winning, thanks to a numerical superiority comparable to that of 1918.

This was a war waged by industrial societies able to mobilize all their men and all their factories. Every citizen contributed to the joint effort, either as worker or soldier. The *levée en masse* decreed by the Convention had become a reality. The effort of organization, including 'the organization of enthusiasm'[1] for which the survivors of the massacre later reproached the old men, was incomparable. This industrial war, waged by civilians in uniform, was to stimulate the pacifist reaction which is a characteristic and not a contradiction of epochs marked by war.

It is possible to regard the second phase of this thirty years' war as belonging, like the first, to the categories of traditional history. The defeated side, which had for so long appeared to be the stronger, retained a keen sense, excessive, perhaps, though comprehensible, of the injustice of the conditions imposed by the victors and made a second attempt.

[1] The phrase is that of Elie Halévy.

41

There could be no true peace unless all rival states were satisfied. Since they were not, what we had was merely a truce. Whatever kind of a government Germany had had, she would have been tempted to break the truce. The ambitions of Hitler's Germany were boundless, and she broke it on the flimsiest of pretexts.

This traditional explanation does not really take account of all the facts. It is true that Jacques Bainville predicted most of the events leading up to the catastrophe of 1939, without taking into account the economic consequences of the war or of the Treaty of Versailles. The successive stages of the tragedy—German rearmament, the re-occupation of the Rhineland, the break-up of France's alliances with the Succession States, the Russo-German pact to partition Poland, the German attack on the West and the rupture of the Russo-German pact—all these have their precedents and are in line with conventional power politics. All the same, it took the great depression of 1929, the millions of workless, and the total disintegration of the political and economic unity of central Europe to convince the millions of Germans that an emotional movement such as National Socialism held out the hope of a future for them. And it took the diabolical genius of a

Hitler to transform this desire for revenge into a monstrous campaign and unparalleled crimes. But though it was inevitable that a war between industrial societies should take the form of what I have called a battle for quantity, the great depression was not an inevitable consequence of the existence of such societies. We now know that it would have been a relatively easy task to limit the extent of the depression. As it was, it was an accident—part of the 'drama'—made possible by the nature of our society. Thirty years ago, it was possible to blame the authors of the Versailles Treaty for ignoring economic necessities. In the period since 1945, an even more irrational settlement than that of 1918 has not, in fact, ruled out prosperity. Between 1918 and 1945, the thirty years' war produced consequences which are still not altogether clear to us and which we are still endeavouring to explain satisfactorily. Were these developments part of the drama or part of the process? Or had they elements of both? And if so, did they belong more to the process or to the drama?

In the perspective of world history—*weltgeschichtlich*, as the Germans would say—these consequences amount to a loss by Europe of her hitherto dominant position. Europe was the centre of world politics. She is now divided into a zone dominated by Soviet Russia and one subject to American influence and protected by American forces. The former colonies have become independent. Industrialization, which was responsible for European superiority, has become, or is in process of becoming, characteristic of the whole human race. Since all sections of humanity now possess, or will shortly possess, the same means of production, will not the ruthless law of quantity henceforth apply in peace as it does in war, and so reduce the old continent to an importance commensurate with its size on the map?

No doubt, what is happening can be explained in the conventional 'dramatic' historical terms, as 'the rape of Europe', or 'the decadence of Europe'. Europeans who have lived through two world wars and experienced the worst that man can do to the honour of his fellow-men, who have seen the end of empires, may be unable to resist the temptation to reflect bitterly on the fragility of historical achievement. But is it essential to look at events in this light? The spread of industrial societies and the unification of the human race are two happenings which were either brought about or speeded up by the thirty years' war, but were they not in any case inevitable? Are they not in accordance with the law of necessity? And is not this dramatic change merely the method of achieving the very result predicted by Auguste Comte, namely, the creation of a single industrial society, uniting, for the first time, the entire human race?

PART III

LET US NOW pause and look at the other facet of this century, namely, that which makes of it a continuous process of accumulation of knowledge and power. Economists and sociologists are now used to studying long-term movements of production and productivity. Thanks to Colin Clark's *Conditions of Economic Progress*, calculations of the rate of growth (of either the national or the *per capita* product) and comparisons of employed labour in each of three sectors have become the accepted method of estimating the development of different economies. But statistics of the national income or of employment clearly reflect the consequences of dramatic happenings as much as they do those of a regular evolution. Industrialization has spread over the whole planet in spite of wars, revolutions and disasters.

This is a fact so self-evident as to require no proof. One illustration will, therefore, be sufficient. Consider, for instance, how differently China and Japan have reacted to the Western threat. In Japan, a minority of the ruling class deliberately set out to bring about the historical mutation, without which the Empire of the Rising Sun

49

would have been condemned to something like servitude. In China, the great majority of the bureaucratic class either failed to grasp the need for, or failed to bring about this necessary mutation and it took a long period of civil wars and the seizure of power by the Communist party for the Chinese State to acquire the strength or the technical capacity to carry out an accelerated programme of industrialization. Since 1890, Asian history has been totally dominated by this gap between the stages of evolution of the two empires. It was the industrial advance achieved by their adoption of Western great-power methods which created in Japan the insane ambition to conquer China. And it was the Sino-Japanese war that gave the Communist party its great opportunity. In both cases, industrialization represents a dramatic phase of the conflict between past and present, between traditionalism and the West.

The working out of this dramatic phase does not merely decide when the phase of scientific evolution will begin and the pace at which it will proceed; it also helps to determine which of a number of possible methods will be the one adopted. It determines which particular social group will take the lead and assume responsibility. In

50

Japan, a class permeated with the spirit of the aristocracy was responsible for bringing about the mutation, a class which sought to integrate national values and Western techniques. In China, it was ultimately a class formed by the Marxist-Leninist ideology and by totalitarian rule which made itself responsible for industrialization and provided leadership for the countless masses. In Russia itself, industrialization had begun during the last quarter of the nineteenth century, when the country was still subject to absolute rule. War and revolution interrupted it and produced a new *élite* which had adopted a Western theory but was opposed to Western liberalism. If the 1914 war had not led to the downfall of Csarism and to the opportunity so long sought by Lenin and his associates, it is conceivable that Russian industrialization might have been achieved by quite different methods, that it might have proceeded at a different pace, and under a different political system. But seen from the viewpoint of 1960, it seems that only the destruction of both the external and the internal unity of her empire could have prevented Russia from becoming the greatest power in Europe. For once nations have at their disposal the same means of production and destruction, then, up to a point, the situation is governed by the law of numbers. But whatever may be our answers, we are certainly justified in asking the following questions: 'What would have happened if Kerensky had eliminated the Bolshevik leaders during the abortive revolution of July 1917?' 'What would have happened if Russia had had two or three decades of peace in which to get over the critical initial phase of industrialization?'

Russia did not have this breathing space, however, and China was not spared the consequences of the ambitions of the more advanced countries of Asia, America and Europe. This did not mean that capitalist economies were inexorably committed to imperialism but rather that industrialization provided both the temptation to conquest and military glory and the means to achieve them. For statesmen and peoples whose thought still ran in traditional grooves, the most important consequence of industrialization was the increase of mobilizable resources, and these were seen as supplementary instruments to be used in traditional activities, rather than as means to the opening-up of a new era.

This is, in a sense, the meeting-point of the concepts of history as usual and necessary history. Are knowledge and power to serve power politics or will they, as Auguste Comte prophesied, replace power politics, and enable a united human race to carry on the only worthwhile battle, namely, that for the mastery of nature and the well-being of mankind? The two great disturbing influences of the twentieth century, Japan and Germany, gave the old-fashioned answer to this modern question. In the view of the masters of these two empires, nothing had changed except the number of soldiers and the efficiency of their weapons. Industry was seen as a means to power and the purpose of power as conquest. Is this still the position today?

At the risk of being thought naïvely presumptious, I would say in reply to this question that the present generation has a better understanding than its predecessors had of the world in which we live, a world whose new features had been intuitively foreseen by the thinkers of the last century.

My optimism is based on a certain number of facts. The first and best known is the revolution which has taken place in the field of armaments. Between 1914 and 1945, the destructive potential was inferior to the productive, or constructive potential. The 1914 armies used weapons less efficient than those that scholars and engineers

53

could have invented and produced, had the best brains been devoted to the task. The 1914 infantry moved at marching speed, and their horse-drawn cannon belonged to the age of tradition. Even armoured divisions and air squadrons did not decisively affect the normal calculations of costs and profits. The revolution came with the nuclear explosive. A war fought with thermo-nuclear bombs would not be a rationally defensible proposition for any belligerent. Since 1945, industry has at last managed to fulfil the first condition of peace through fear of war, an objective announced prematurely by so many writers. This does not mean that peace is now assured. It merely means that war can no longer be the continuation of a policy carried on by other means. Unless one of the belligerents is much less vulnerable than the rest, thermo-nuclear warfare can occur only as the result of either an accident or a misunderstanding.

In addition, world opinion today understands more clearly than ever before the facts of modern economic life and its potentialities for peace. The possible causes of conflict between classes or between nations now seem less important than the things that make for interdependence.

Of course, there is nothing fundamentally new

in all this. For centuries, liberal economists have been proclaiming that trade benefits both sides, that the essential feature of the economic system is exchange and that wars and conquest are always sterile and frequently ruinous for all concerned.

What is new is that these convictions, formerly held only by a few, are now spreading, thanks to recent knowledge. Western Germany occupies a territory smaller than France, and has been obliged to absorb some ten million refugees, yet she is enjoying unprecedented prosperity. For her, the price of defeat has been, not poverty, as hitherto, but prosperity. Western Europe as a whole, including Great Britain, has lost colonies, power, diplomatic prestige, yet she has achieved an unprecedented level of production and productivity.

In the Thirties, the West, obsessed by the great depression, thought in quasi-Marxist terms, looked for markets and ended up by concluding that lack of markets meant economic paralysis, then or later. Today, the West has realized with surprise that, in spite of recessions and temporary halts, expansion creates markets, of itself and for itself, as economists had always maintained. The progress achieved by the Soviet Union through a rigidly planned system, by federal Germany through a relatively free economic system, and by other European countries through methods combining both principles, has discredited so-called doctrinal quarrels in many people's minds. The scientific, social and human conditions of expansion—the number of technicians, the incentives to progress that drive *entrepreneurs* and administrators, the spontaneous or forced acceptance of change by the masses—these are now considered more important than methods of government. The emphasis is on the factors making for economic expansion in general, instead of on the specific characteristics of a particular regime.

By the same process, ideologies are also becoming discredited and tending to lose their emotional effectiveness. In the West, and perhaps even in the Soviet Union, men no longer think of one regime as being imperialist or exploiting, and of another as being peaceful and just. All regimes are thought of as imperfect and none is immune from injustice, none is subject to the law of impoverishment. The most fervent opponents of Communism will concede the rapid expansion of the Soviet economy and the rise in the standard of living of the masses. The most fervent opponents of the liberal West or of capitalism no longer pretend that there has been any serious economic crisis since 1945 and admit that the exploited proletariat has never had it so good.

Does this mean that the industrial society to which Auguste Comte looked forward and which is now, in different ways, in process of formation is in reality a prototype, and that humanity is now becoming socially uniform as well as diplomatically unified? Such a conclusion would be premature. The dawn of universal history is, I think, about to break and universal history will present a number of original features compared with provincial, national history, or with the culture of the past six thousand years. But nothing indicates that it will cease to be dramatic.

What exactly do I mean by the expression universal history? First, unification within the field in which diplomacy works. China and Japan, the Soviet Union and the United States, France and Great Britain, Germany and Italy, India and Ghana—all these states today form part of a single system. What happens on the Chinese coasts has repercussions on the relations between Europe and the United States, or between the United States and the Soviet Union. Never have so many states recognized the reciprocal rights of others to existence. Never have Europe and Asia, Africa and America, felt so close to each other. Where, formerly, great states limited their field of activity to Europe or to Asia, the great states of today, that is, for the time being, the United States and the Soviet Union, have a field of activity covering five continents. It is a commonplace to say that transport and means of communication have abolished distances. The accumulation of the instruments of knowledge and power in states which are also continents is also a condition of planetary diplomacy, of the changed scale of power.

With diplomatic unification there goes the universal spread of certain forms of technical and economic organization. No community anxious to survive can afford deliberately to slow down the development of what the Marxists call the forces of production—the rationalization of labour and the growth of technical equipment. How can we reject what provides power and prosperity? And so the visitor is struck by the spectacle of the same factories, the same aerodromes, the same machines, from Tokyo to Paris, from Pekin to Rio de Janeiro. The same words—capitalism, communism, imperialism, dollar, rouble—ring in his ears as soon as he enters into conversation with an intellectual or a politician. A traveller might reach the superficial conclusion that the human race lives in a single world in the sense that the same ideas as well as the same machines are found the world over.

Such an impression, however, would be to a great extent illusory. Whatever the degree of diplomatic unification, humanity is, today, as divided as ever diplomatic systems were in the past. At the heart of Europe, two coalitions confront each other, and more and more states boast of their refusal to be attached to either one or the other. The relations between the Soviet Union and China are, to some extent, wrapped in mystery. The United Nations presents a symbolic forum to the spokesmen of states in the universal era, but most of the speeches express, not the real personality of the weaker and therefore powerless states, but the ideology which they have adopted in order to give themselves the feeling that they are playing a part in human history.

It is possible that the conventional classifications inherited from our provincial past are less important than the classifications of an epoch in which a new type of society is becoming dominant. Of the two forms of industrial society, the Soviet and the Western, one at least claims sole validity for all men at all times. The incarnation in two historic regions and two states of the two ideologies characteristic of the West has been accompanied by a provisional classification of peoples valid at least over ten-year periods, though, in the long term only provisional—into rich and poor, into those who possess practically everything and those who possess practically nothing, into those called under-developed and those already reaping the fruits of productivity. For a human race in process of becoming unified, inequality between peoples plays the role formerly played by inequality between classes. The condition of the masses differs from continent to continent and from country to country more today than it has ever done. And as the consciousness of this inequality becomes more widespread, people cease to be resigned to poverty, to accept their fate.

In the different sections that make up the unified human race, causes of conflict are no longer hidden behind some spiritual unity. For unification is henceforth based solely on material, technical or economic factors. The power to produce, to destroy, to communicate, has conquered and abolished the obstacles formerly presented by oceans and mountains. Men who neither worship the same god, nor respect the same customs nor think in the same categories now find their spiritual unity only in a handful of expressions which they owe to vague ideologies inherited from nineteenth-century European theories. Never before have states belonging to the same diplomatic system differed as they differ today. Never before have people involved in a common enterprise been so disunited on fundamental issues.

For ten years or more we have been obsessed by the gulf that exists between the Communist and the free worlds. How could we fail to be so, with Soviet armies stationed 125 miles from the Rhine, and Soviet propaganda claiming that the ultimate triumph of Communism is inevitable the world over—claiming, in other words, that the West must choose between death by violence or death by inanition.

Nor is this all. The clash between the two *blocs* is twofold. There is both rivalry for power and ideological competition. There is foreign war with some of the characteristics of civil war. Economic planning by a proletariat in control of the State and aiming at equality and plenty, whether it is or is not achieved by the Soviet Union, is a Western dream, a Utopia in which reality has been stood on its head, and which has dominated Western politics, if not Western philosophy, for decades. It may well be that the Russia of the orthodox Church and Byzantium, and the Russia whose monolithic traditions are an inheritance from oriental bureaucracy, belong to a civilization totally different from that of Western Europe. But the Russia which claims to be Marxist and Socialist belongs to Western civilization, at least in her vocabulary and her claim to have actually achieved what the best among European reformers had preached as the objectives of the entire human race.

It is possible, however, that the conflict is now becoming less acute. The leaders of both *blocs* are well aware of the irrationality of a war to the death, waged with atomic and thermo-nuclear weapons. Even the most doctrinaire are gradually being forced to recognize the resemblances between the techniques of organization of industries functioning on different legal bases. There is, of course, still plenty of room for genuine controversy. Different methods of government, property systems, methods of controlling the national economy, all these produce systems which differ also in their ways of life and thought. Let us not be guilty of the error of some Marxists who, on the basis of partial resemblances between productive forces and methods of labour organization, refuse to recognize the real impact of the economic system on political communities. This is no less serious an error than the former Communist exaggeration out of all measure of the influence of economic systems, the one being held to ensure peace, equality and abundance, the other to lead inevitably to imperialism, exploitation and poverty in the midst of an accumulation of excess wealth. These two conflicting myths are equally false. Let us not yield to the temptation to create yet a third, perhaps less objectionable, but with no more truth in it. There is no more reason to believe that mature industrial societies will necessarily achieve moral unity than that they will necessarily disagree with each other. Even if, as seems likely, they come more and more to resemble each other, there is no guarantee that they will get on with each other. How many of the great wars of history look in retrospect, like family quarrels!

Indeed, even if we accept what is now the fashionable thesis that the two great powers will each undergo a gradual conversion, it would still be wrong to conclude that, even in an age of universal history, the problem of unity can be reduced merely to one aspect of the relations between the United States and the Soviet Union, or even to that aspect of their relations which is concerned with the difference between, on the one hand, a system of economic planning under the direction of a single party and, on the other, a semi-liberal and multi-party system. The two other decisive factors that I have just mentioned, inequality of development and diversity of customs and beliefs, must also be taken into account. The first is a historic survival and is characteristic of a transition period. But even if we assume that the African and Asian peoples will eventually cease to be backward (and this cannot happen in the immediate future) a correct balance between population and territorial frontiers can be achieved only if the growth of population is controlled. And since the natural methods of limiting the population (famine and epidemics), have ceased to be effective, such control can be achieved only by the conscious will of individuals or communities. If nations do not achieve a reasonable limitation of their populations, then numerical disparities and differences in the standard of living will recur perpetually, and bring poverty and incitements to violence in their train.

The second decisive factor may have even more far-reaching repercussions. If human history is to become universal, men will have to learn rational control, not merely of their biological instincts, but also of their social passions. The more men of different races, religions and customs find themselves living in one world, the more they will have to learn to treat each other with tolerance and mutual respect. They will have to recognize the human rights of all, and refrain from ambitions of conquest or domination. This is a commonplace to which it is easy to subscribe in theory. But, on reflection, it will be evident that it is a requirement that demands of mankind a quite new moral quality. For it is what men hold sacred that divides men most. A pagan or a Jew who remains unconverted to Christianity is a challenge. Can the man who knows nothing of the God of the salvationist religions be a fellow-man, or is he someone with whom we can feel nothing in common? Whatever our answer, it is with him that the new spiritual community must be established—as the superstructure, or the foundation, of the material community now arising from the scientific, technical and economic unity that historical necessity is imposing on men who are still more conscious of what divides than of what unites them.

It took the tragedy of two world wars to unify the diplomatic spheres. It took successive revolutions in France, Russia and China to achieve the spread of industrial development. It was violence that forced a way through, and the path is strewn with millions of innocent victims. The trick of reason, (*die List der Vernunft*), put forward by the disciples of Bossuet, Hegel and Marx, has been costly in terms of suffering and blood. Nothing justifies the conclusion that all this belongs to the past and that henceforth evolution can proceed rationally without drama. It may be that universal history will differ in this respect from the provincial history of past ages. But this is only a hope based solely on faith.

THIS SOMEWHAT AMBIGUOUS statement is probably all that can be said by way of conclusion within the framework of the present outline. Those of our contemporaries who subscribe to philosophies of history place their emphasis on one of two related concepts of historical development. Optimistic philosphers, whether of Marxist or liberal inspiration, see the future in terms of an endless process of accumulation of knowledge and power. They see the human race as sharing equitably, through either fair exchange or rational planning, the benefits of progress achieved by the genius of scholars or of technicians. Pessimistic philosophers, such as Spengler, for example, point out the resemblances between the disasters which have overwhelmed past cultures and those that we have witnessed in the course of the twentieth century. They see Western civilization as dying, just as classical culture died, thanks to wars and revolutions, thanks to tentacular urban agglomerations and rootless masses, thanks to the over-refinement of powerless *élites* and the triumph of money or of technical skill. Is not a Europe which has lost her empires already decadent?

Does not the possession by other races of the instruments by which the domination of the white minority has been maintained signify the inevitable decline of Europe?

Both optimists and pessimists, however, misunderstand certain characteristics of our epoch, certain potentialities of the universal age. Looked at in the light of past experience, present-day happenings in the old continent justify gloomy forebodings. What will yesterday's Great Powers—England, France, Germany, with their fifty million populations in quest of material well-being—look like beside states which are continents and count their populations by hundreds of millions? Has not the loss of their empires deprived the European nations of their historic personality, so to speak, and must they not, therefore, give up hope of greatness?

This traditional approach is perhaps anachronistic, for, in our century, domination has more often than not brought financial liabilities instead of profits. Rationally organized labour is both the source and the measure of wealth. As Europe looks at a world now in the process of adopting a type of civilization that she created, she need not, necessarily, regard herself as the victim of her own triumph. Greatness and military strength are no longer inseparable, both because the Great Powers can no longer use armed force without risking reprisals which will result in their own destruction, and also because it is no longer essential for any society to dominate another in order to provide a good life for its citizens.

Europe has, thus, two reasons for refusing to regard herself as decadent. It was her achievements, and later her military follies, which were responsible for bringing humanity to the threshold of the universal age. When men no longer need to tyrannize over each other in order to be able to exploit natural resources, Europe can still be great if she conforms to the spirit of the new age by helping other peoples to cure the infantile diseases of modernism. If she can apply her principles at home and still have a task to perform abroad, why should she continue to feel a bitterness which her recent past may explain, but which future prospects do not justify? Never before have men had so many reasons for ceasing to slaughter each other. Never before have they had so many reasons for feeling that they are all involved in the same adventure. This does not necessarily mean that the age of universal history will be peaceful. If man, in the abstract, is, as we know, a rational being, does it follow that men in the real world will behave rationally?

After a long and circuitous journey I have finally reached a position which popular wisdom would accept. I have moved from Hegel and the trick of reason to Candide and the language of Voltaire. When philosophy (or sociology) and common sense join hands, is that to be regarded as a tribute to common sense or as a proof of the wisdom of philosophy?